W9-BMA-584

Tyrannosaurus Rex

by Wil Mara

Content Consultant
Gregory M. Erickson, PhD
Paleontologist
The Florida State University
Tallahassee, Florida

Reading Consultant
Jeanne Clidas
Reading Specialist

Children's Press®
An Imprint of Scholastic Inc.
New York Toronto London Auckland Sydney
Mexico City New Delhi Hong Kong
Danbury, Connecticut

Library of Congress Cataloging-in-Publication Data
Mara, Wil.
  Tyrannosaurus rex/by Wil Mara.
    p. cm.—(Rookie read-about dinosaurs)
  Includes bibliographical references and index.
  ISBN-13: 978-0-531-20861-8 (lib. bdg.)   ISBN-10: 0-531-20861-3 (lib. bdg.)
  ISBN-13: 978-0-531-20930-1 (pbk.)   ISBN-10: 0-531-20930-X (pbk.)
  1. Tyrannosaurus rex—Juvenile literature. I. Title.
  QE862.S3M3317 2012
  567.912'9—dc23   2011032220

1 2 3 4 5 6 7 8 9 10 R 21 20 19 18 17 16 15 14 13 12

Photographs © 2012: Black Hills Institute of Geological Research, Inc./Larry
Shaffer: 28, 29; iStockphoto/Mike Kiev: 14, 31 top right; Media Bakery: cover; Photo
Researchers: 18 (Chris Butler), 20 (Mark Garlick), 4, 31 top left (Mark Hallett
Paleoart), 16 (Warren Photographic); Shutterstock, Inc.: 22, 31 bottom right
(Chris Harvey), 24, 25 (DM7), 12, 31 bottom left (De Agostini), 6 (National
Geographic); The Image Works/The Natural History Museum: 8, 26, 27.

TABLE OF CONTENTS

THE KING OF THE DINOSAURS

Tyrannosaurus rex (tih-ran-uh-SAWR-uss REHX) was one of the biggest dinosaurs ever.

Babies came from eggs.
Even a baby was as big as
a large cat!

It ate other animals. It did not eat plants.

BIG . . . VERY BIG!

Tyrannosaurus rex was as heavy as an elephant. It was as long as a school bus.

FAST RUNNER

Tyrannosaurus rex had small front legs.

The back legs were huge
and strong.

It walked with its head low.
Its tail stuck out.

Tyrannosaurus rex was big. But it could run faster than most other dinosaurs.

DINNERTIME

Tyrannosaurus rex ate other animals. Sometimes it hunted them. Other times it ate animals that had already died.

Tyrannosaurus rex had small teeth in the front of its mouth. They were very sharp.

The teeth in the back were very big. Some were as long as bananas.

The Tyrannosaurus rex had strong jaws too.

It ate the meat of other animals.
It could also eat all the bones!

DINOSAUR BONES

Scientists found Tyrannosaurus rex bones. They built a skeleton from the bones. It is in a museum.

Can you find the teeth in this skeleton? Can you count how many toes were on the front legs?

TRY THIS! Go back in the book with your child and look at the illustration that shows the Tyrannosaurus rex front and back teeth (pp 24–25). You can remind your child that the T. rex teeth were very sharp so they could tear apart other animals for food. Compare other parts of the dinosaur skeleton with the illustrations to help your child review what he read in the book.

- The name Tyrannosaurus rex means "tyrant king."

- The largest Tyrannosaurus rex was found in South Dakota.

Visit this Scholastic web site for more information on the Tyrannosaurus rex: **www.factsfornow.scholastic.com**

WORDS YOU KNOW

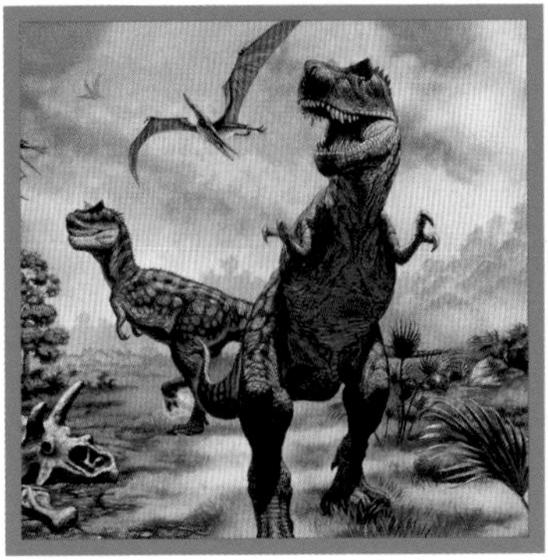

Tyrannosaurus rex

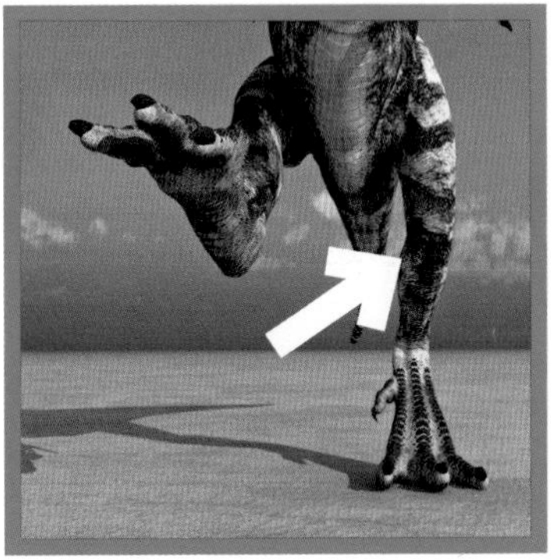

legs

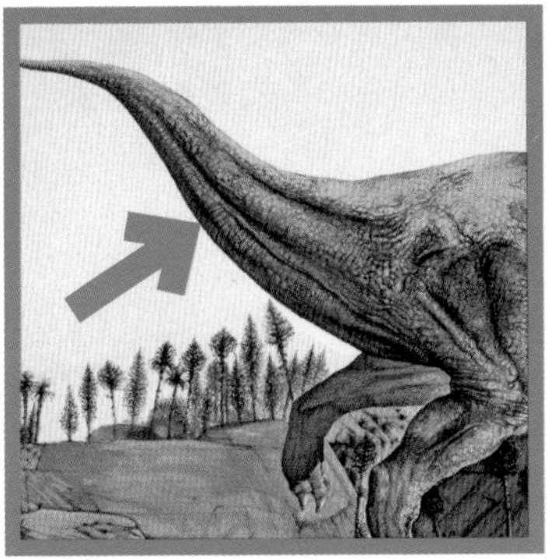

tail

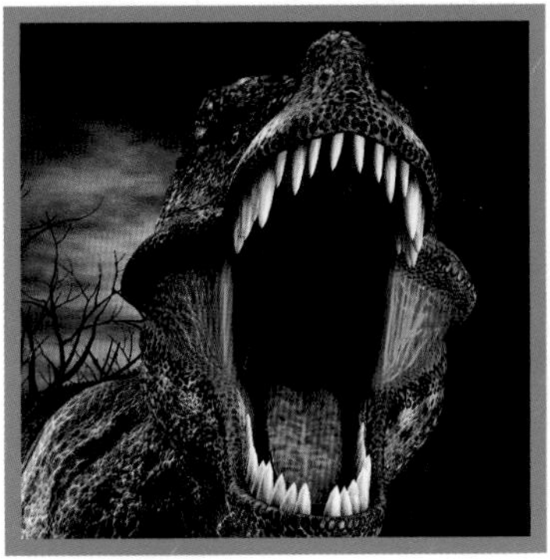

teeth

Index

Learn More!

You can learn more about the Tyrannosaurus rex at:

www.childrensmuseum.org/ themuseum/dinosphere/profiles/ bucky.html

About the Author

Wil Mara is the award-winning author of more than 100 books, many of them educational titles for young readers. More information about his work can be found at *www.wilmara.com*.